PLAYBACK+
eed • Pitch • Balance • Loop

AUDIO
ACCESS
INCLUDED

HORN

T0070793

Audio arrangements by Peter Deneff

To access audio visit:
www.halleonard.com/mylibrary
Enter Code
1194-9703-6819-0345

ISBN 978-1-5400-2138-0

HAL•LEONARD®

7777 W. BLUEMOUND RD. P.O. BOX 13819 MILWAUKEE, WI 53213

In Australia Contact:
Hal Leonard Australia Pty. Ltd.
4 Lentara Court
Cheltenham, Victoria, 3192 Australia
Email: ausadmin@halleonard.com.au

Visit Hal Leonard Online at
www.halleonard.com

EVERYONE KNOWS JUANITA

from COCO

HORN

Music by GERMAINE FRANCO
Lyrics by ADRIAN MOLINA

MUCH NEEDED ADVICE

from COCO

Horn

Music by MICHAEL GIACCHINO
and GERMAINE FRANCO
Lyrics by ADRIAN MOLINA

LA LLORONA
from COCO

HORN

Traditional Mexican Folksong
Arranged by GERMAINE FRANCO

PROUD CORAZÓN
from COCO

Music by GERMAINE FRANCO
Lyrics by ADRIAN MOLINA

HORN

REMEMBER ME
(Ernesto de la Cruz)
from COCO

Horn

Words and Music by KRISTEN ANDERSON-LOPEZ
and ROBERT LOPEZ

UN POCO LOCO
from COCO

HORN

Music by GERMAINE FRANCO
Lyrics by ADRIAN MOLINA

THE WORLD ES MI FAMILIA
from COCO

HORN

Music by GERMAINE FRANCO
Lyrics by ADRIAN MOLINA